INKED

CORINNA MCCLANAHAN SCHROEDER

Corinna McClanahan Schroeder

Texas Review Press
Huntsville, Texas

FIRST EDITION

Requests for permission to acknowledge material from this work should be sent to:

Permissions
Texas Review Press
English Department
Sam Houston State University
Huntsville, TX 77341-2146

Many thanks to the editors and staff of the following journals, in which these poems first appeared:

32 Poems: "Years Later, I See My Old Self Stumbling Down the Street"
Blackbird: "Haibun for the Grantham Station Platform" and "Ritual with Seven Selves"
Cave Wall: "Maududo Lessons" (published as "Miss Ohio Does Maududo")
Cellpoems: "It's not the bed that's a boat"
Cimarron Review: "To the Heroine"
The Common: "Instructions for Return" (published as "Miss Ohio Teaches You to Drive")
Copper Nickel: "On the Last Day of Our Wild Year"
diode: "Ordering Work" (published as "Loveland Library")
Georgetown Review: "Odyssey"
The Gettysburg Review: "Gathering" and "Mating Rituals of the Bioluminescent"
Glass: A Journal of Poetry: "We Were Learning to be Silent Together—"
Hayden's Ferry Review: "On Not Kissing Whitney"
Heron Tree: "Holding"
Iron Horse Literary Review: "Whiskey Haircut" (published as "Lessons from a Whiskey Haircut")
Linebreak: "Lake Ouachita, Late Summer"
Michigan Quarterly Review: "Exposure Time"
New Madrid: "At Skegness" and "Jesuit Anatomy for Freshman" (published as "Freshman Anatomy")
Pebble Lake Review: "You Tell Me of the Winters in Laramie"
Poemeleon: "Reading Edith Hamilton, Ninth Grade"
Poet Lore: "The Stage Carpenter's Wife"
Shenandoah: "'A House upon the Height—'"
Thrush Poetry Journal: "Inked," "Snow," and "Vanishing Point"
The Xavier Review: "Storm Watching in the First Year of Marriage"

"Mating Rituals of the Bioluminescent" also appeared on *Poetry Daily*.

Cover Design: Nancy Parsons, Graphic Design Group
Cover Art: Brooke Sharp, *Paisley Bird Silhouette*, 2014. Pen on Canvas, 20 x 26cm.
Author Photograph: Matthew Schroeder

Library of Congress Cataloging-in-Publication Data

Schroeder, Corinna McClanahan, 1985- author.
 [Poems. Selections]
 Inked / Corinna McClanahan Schroeder. ~ Edition: first.
   pages cm
 ISBN 978-1-68003-059-4 (pbk. : alk. paper)
 I. Title.
 PS3619.C46465A6 2015
 811'.6~dc23
                              2015018458

ACKNOWLEDGEMENTS

Heartfelt gratitude to my teachers: to Carol Muske-Dukes, for her editorial insight and belief in this project, and to David St. John and Mark Irwin at the University of Southern California; to Beth Ann Fennelly, Ann Fisher-Wirth, and Gary Short for helping me shape and revise many of these poems when I was their student at the University of Mississippi; and to Bill Baer, Rob Griffith, and Paul Bone for early lessons and encouragement at the University of Evansville. Endless thanks, too, to the many writers who've influenced my work, who've inspired me, whose friendship I hold dear—and especially to Michelle Brittan, Danielle Sellers, Heather Matesich Cousins, Joan Schadt Biddle, Sarah Vap, Todd Fredson, and Diana Arterian for their help in bringing this book to its final form, and to Katie Darby Mullins, Travis Blakenship, Emileigh Barnes, Anya Groner, Jimmy Kimbrell, Alicia Casey, and Chris Hayes for their generous feedback on drafts of these poems.

Special thanks to William Virgil Davis for selecting this book for the X. J. Kennedy Poetry Prize and to Paul Ruffin and the staff of Texas Review Press for making this book happen.

Thanks also to John and Renée Grisham, under whose generous fellowship at the University of Mississippi this manuscript was started, and to the University of Southern California for a Wallis Annenberg Endowed Fellowship, which helped me complete it.

And, finally, a thank you to my family. To my parents, for their love and support and for their friendship, which I hold dear. To Alyssa and Kegan, for being my oldest and best friends. And to Matthew, for his love and light and unwavering belief in me.

For Matthew

CONTENTS

*   *   *

INKED

"Power . . . resides in the moment of transition."
—Emerson, *"Self-Reliance"*

*   *   *

INKED

I went alone, bared the scroll of my back
to Big Richard whose fingers spelled T-H-I-S

I-S I-T when he fisted his hands together.
"Won't hurt," he grunted, and I wanted to say,

"Richard, I'm here for hurt." He pressed the gun
to me, its needles thrusting in and out faster

than I could separate. Henna-colored ink pulsed
under my skin, and I felt the shape take form,

the circle spiral in. Sweat under my breasts,
on the back of my neck. My body gave itself

to needles. My vision blistered with light.
At home, I peeled the dressing away

to stare at the welt—to remind myself
what the body can do, what the body can say.

ORDERING WORK

On school nights, through labyrinthine rows,
Dewey's decimals guided the cart's wheel-spin.
Near-sighted old men came in to read *The Sun*,

The Enquirer, *The Times*. Their wives pecked
at the books on tape. Children spun through
the spinning racks while their mothers pocketed

romance in paper bags. There were the yellers,
unhappy with fines. Those who couldn't find
what they wanted, those who didn't know what to find.

At dusk, the lonesome man who slunk through the aisles
like yolk on a skillet's shine. I didn't mind
my ordering work. I breathed the books, the older

the better. Oily, woody, spiced like mushrooms
or vanilla. When the librarians weren't looking,
I pulled hardbacks from the top shelf, popped

their spines. On the inside cover's spread,
the brown spots of an avocado's inner fruit.
Mold bloomed no matter what we did. I haunted

that floor, so motionless that the lights cut out.
The millions of printed pages raised my hair,
and I waited in the opacity, glad of it. Each night,

I hung the "Closed" sign, then braced for the metal slam
of books falling from the drop box to the receiving bin.
Sometimes, I think, all night they tumbled in.

READING EDITH HAMILTON, NINTH GRADE

Girls' legs splayed by boars

    and bulls and swans.
        A hoof jammed
into the tight   of a back,
       a beak fastening
around a neck.

    Girls sealed inside laurels and reeds.
      One girl, even, pulled
          into a stranger's car

    and the mother left behind,
    poppies wilting.

That winter, between bells,
       upperclassmen boys
   jostled me in the halls.

Their smell sharpened
       to musk.
Their shoulders spread,
    eyes dark   as drowned stones.

And that ripple
   in the pit of me.

     In the parking lot,
every day at 2:55, engine rev
    and muffler breath,
       tires peeling out.

I stood on the sidewalk,
   coat zipped high.

MAUDUDO LESSONS

I let older men flip me onto mats. They did it
gently, like they might hurt me.

I was serious. Parry, backfist, wristlock, knuckle punch.
I didn't know how sixteen

I looked or was. Outside, headlights swished the weeknight
darkness like the energy

we moved made manifest. The instructor complimented my kicks—
front, roundhouse, and side.

During exercises, I aimed at my mirrored self. Planted foot,
bent knee. Focused extension,

full release. I met that gaze. Some nights we talked meditation,
chokeholds, *qi*. We learned action's

two ways. What's pushed doesn't have to yield. *Use the opponent's force,*
the instructor explained, *don't muscle*

against it but turn it back. I can't say this lesson stuck with me,
busy in boys' backseats,

but I liked the idea that I could return what was thrown at me.
One night I asked how

to escape a straddling. Didn't mention the wet grass or how I'd wished
I were home safe in my sheets.

Elbow the crook of his arm, buck, lock that arm over your knee. Break
if necessary. It sounded easy.

I never tried. That night, at the end of class, our starched uniforms creased, we recited the student creed—

I am developing myself in a positive manner. We bowed to ourselves long and deep.

TO THE HEROINE

Keep your braid in the tower already.
  Nobody believes you mistook
    the prince's call for the witch.
      A baritone's no cackle.

    You think I don't know you?
    I know the tangle of each morning,
  my fingers thick in unrelenting curl.
I know the dull ache of bearing

a braid too long. Our gold hair glistens
  in its death. You've never seen a man
    except for him—so why the hurry,
      the *bring me scarves for a ladder and I'll leave?*

    There are many square jaws, tapered
    hips, taut hamstrings. This one,
  though, was creeping in the woods,
eavesdropping on your vocal scales,

waiting for the key—*Rapunzel, Rapunzel,*
  let down your hair. What, you think
    I haven't known wait? Every daughter
    has a bedroom she'd like to escape,

    but as much as this masonry
    keeps you in, it keeps the risk away.
  It's desert ahead. A shorn head.
Two spoonfuls in the center of you.

That's right, twins. And the prince—
  he'll follow still, blind, thorn scars
    across his eyelids. Bear out
      this interim with all the other girls

who smolder under mother-roofs.
For now, be glad you're safe.
Stash the scarves he brought—
you can lower yourself.

JESUIT ANATOMY FOR FRESHMEN

In lab, we picked stiff, plastic-wrapped cats
from the stack. I named mine Boots for the fur tufts
left on his feet. The formaldehyde stung my eyes

as I scissored his breastbone, pulled apart ribs,
and pinned his skin to flanks. He was cold beneath
my gloves, his eyes marbled glass. Our heavy text

offered diagrams for each system—but I recognized
nothing, the body unfathomable broken apart,
my fingers already smelling like the skin's underside.

I spent every Tuesday that fall trying to name his parts:
first the yellow adipose tissue like cottage cheese,
the tarsus and sacrum bones, caudal tail vertebrae

like a bracelet chain. Then the gray muscle—teres major
and linea alba, tagged and mislabeled. I hated those slow
surgeries with a blunt scalpel, the instructor pacing,

the other students all chatter, and me in the back row
prodding Boots's body. I stayed afterhours
to finish alone. Downstairs, med students worked

through the thin-veined night in the cadaver morgue.
By Thanksgiving, we'd covered the ribbed straw
of trachea, deflated balloons of small intestines,

the tough brown fruit of liver. Our final:
subclavian arteries infused with red dye, the superior
vena cava colored blue. The vascular lines

required a steady hand, but the fine, white nerves
called for a saint's persistence, slow breath:
brachial plexus underneath the pecs, phrenic

of the diaphragm, sciatic which descends the thigh.
The nerves like gossamer, and still, each one
a bundle of something smaller. I couldn't dig

deep enough, though I tried. Last lab, I tucked Boots
into his disposal bag and walked outside where stars
broke like a rash across an unpatterned sky.

ON NOT KISSING WHITNEY

We lived in the attic of a frat house behind
a peeling red door, behind the scratched

initials of all the boys who'd lived there
all the years before. Our lofted beds

floated like boats. At night, the ones
who'd stayed for summer poured us cups

of warm beer. They came to smell
the shampoo scent, to see our underwear

dangling from the beams, waiting
to be touched. When they left, we snuck

to the quad to smoke Virginia Slims—
wands, long and thin. Crabgrass

scratched the skin of our ankle bones.
She talked sex, bawdy as any man I knew,

and I didn't miss home in that lull that felt
like years when we were wordless, kissing

cigarettes, terrified of how the lonesome space
loosed us to wander like trespassers—

or prisoners. All the while, the peonies
unclenched their blooms in the fevered air.

YEARS LATER, I SEE MY OLD SELF
STUMBLING DOWN THE STREET

A scent I haven't worn in years—
McCormick Vodka from the plastic jug.
Stiletto-shake and curls straight, her hips
like knobs beneath her cocktail dress, she shouts
to her gaggle that she wants to dance. She laughs
her throatiest laugh. The darkness holds her
like she holds her cigarette—ready to drop it
for the next.
              Darling, watch the cherry. Keep
your clutch on your wrist. Don't let a stranger pour
your drinks. But you're me. You'll shoot them fast,
your thumb a mixing spoon, your eyes half-moons.
No more, no more, you'll lie, even as you tip
your punch-red mouth towards the toilet's bowl,
no one to smooth your ruffles back in place.

INDIANA, WHILE IT LASTED

She drove them out of town at dusk.
Past the fluorescent lights of truck stops,

their twitching signs. Whole fields of gold
tassels undulated in the wind, an accordion

of small birds. That's how things were.
A tractor path between cloying rows of corn.

The boy's hand drumming his thigh
until they thumbed for buttons and straps.

The metal buckle dug its jaw into her knee,
and she touched his skinny shoulders,

the sparse field of hair along the sternum.
Gas station sodas seeped through their paper cups,

purple light still grazing the west.
A late summer then of thirst and distant passing

cattle rigs. She drove them home,
her shaking hands steady on the wheel.

WE WERE LEARNING TO BE SILENT TOGETHER—

my fingers pinching the radio knob,
  the vents' hot blast and the window cracked,
    his headlights' narrow arc. He sped because,

four months in, he knew I liked it. Hungover
  with winter, I wanted his thick, chapped hands
    at ten and two. Gas petal velocity, a throatful

of gelid air, the hollow screech the window let inside.
  The tempered glass slicked our slack-eyed selves,
    mousy hair all shine. Beyond, snow fell like ash.

In winter, Indiana's wasteland—the umber soil
  raked hard and clean of crops, frosted in that nighttime hour.
    Clapton took an FM wave. Even into the empty exit lane,

we accelerated. He turned the wheel according
  to the ramp's clover shape, but too late—the car skipped
    ice and didn't slow. Our mouths opened, noiseless Os.

ON THE LAST DAY OF OUR WILD YEAR

December light is the light of the underworld,
    each beam a thread to be pulled.
  You drive 57 which uppercuts Illinois's jaw
as I watch salt streaks smear by, thrilled
    with the notion of January—Janus,
      god of the doorway. We'll be good this year.
        The Mississippi slides like steel wool
beneath us, the bridge buzzing our velocity.
    One threshold crossed, I thumb your thigh.

  When I wake, you are braking to the shoulder.
  "Speed trap," you say, "they're pulling me over."
    They run your license—old photo
    of the down-cheeked boy you were.
      I drag a cigarette when two officers
pull you from the car, tell you *warrant,*
    extradition. Best magic trick,
  they take you from me. The old state
wants you back, and I don't have the key.
    Our champagne chills in the trunk.

    I trail the patrol car, eyes trained
      on your vague backseat form.
At the county jail, they take your pocketknife,
    your watch, the socks I washed.
  The lady behind the window tells me no one's
  getting out till after the first. Outside, I call
    your mother who'll be dead within four months.
    She swallows my news, announces
      her tumors into the phone.
You don't know. My snagged breaths rise.

In the only hotel nearby, I watch shadows
linger and pass in the inch-gap between
my locked door and the linoleum. *I need him back,*
    I mouth to the girl the mirror holds—
    who's not my other half. Thin
        and sallow-faced, her eyes black discs.
We were greedy, we're sorry. Daylight dissolves
    in the cup of night. I fall asleep before the clock
reads twelve. When I wake to a muted TV,
January's there, two-faced, knowing everything.

*   *   *

RITUAL WITH SEVEN SELVES

The washer fills like a well, and she casts
them in, delicates zipped into netted bags,
buttons threaded through their loops.
Cold waters purl and rise, bubbles frothing
like spells. The safety latch long broken,
she watches her selves slosh, each one rising up,
then drowning. Red dress, red dress
of a goose-bumped night and an endless goblet
of wine that made her spill all her best lines
like scarves from the jester's sleeve. Dark hands
reach up from the well's underside. Float
of sweater, its noose of a neck that held her head
in place, her heavy tongue. Her mouth
was a broken bell that day. Cloak worn against
the rain when she went walking in the woods,
the trees wet-barked and no pebbles dropped
to lead her home. Jeans, too, mud-cuffed
and stretched beyond shape. Backless top
in which she swallowed mushrooms and milk.
Mermaids filled the sink, their scales coarse as salt,
and wolves came to the door and knocked.
Flash of diaphanous legs amid the many haggard
sleeves—stockings ripped by the charcoal cat
she keeps. Nightgown, last, of turbulent dreams,
of a poisoned Red Delicious and spindles that spin
a girl to sleep. She leans her head and breathes.
Let the waters ravage each seam. Let every sock
be a step in reverse, every stripe the sure hand
of a clock. Let the basket spin to oblivion,
the water's last drop flung free, the well run clean.

SNOW

She would know, she tells herself. If something were to happen—were to have happened—she would feel it, would have already felt it. All afternoon, he was only across town stocking amber bottles on dusty shelves, the men coming in, released early from their shifts, and stomping their boots on the mat. Now he is long off work. But there would have been a sign, she would have heard a wreck coming in her body, no matter how far. His body is a knowledge, and she knows. The tiny scar underneath his beard, his index finger and palm just long enough to encircle her wrist. His narrow hips, and his chest, next to her in bed, a slab of wood. Outside, snow falls and falls, insulating the house. And still—she would have felt it—he does not—she would know—come home.

STORM WATCHING IN THE
FIRST YEAR OF MARRIAGE

Sirens break the susurrous hour along its seam.
3:30 a.m. and my husband's still grinding

his teeth, still grinding out his sleep.
The one-tone scream sluices our box fan's

hummingbird wing. It's probably just
impending thunder, some cumulonimbus

crowd along the Arkansas border, but I slip
from bed. In the living room, the cable's out.

The crape myrtles thrash, the wind picking
at the door's lock. I step outside as if

I can lick a finger and catch the storm's
direction. My parents used to pluck me

from tangled sheets, carry my siblings and me
to cellar cover. Just another sleepover

for me. I could sleep through anything.
Now a thumbnail moon loiters overhead,

lightning in the west. The white strobes rend
the night to pieces, and in the salt-tinged whip

of wind, an armada of clouds rolls in—
plum-bruised hulls, billowing masts.

The county sirens panic-ring. I hold
the balcony rail, but as fast as it gathered,

the cloud mass swerves north toward
Holly Springs. It's no relief. Nights stretch

ahead of me, no longer the dreamer
but the woken, the watcher, the guard.

THE STAGE CARPENTER'S WIFE

First the thin and waxy blueprints unscrolled
across the kitchen table. Compass, ruler,

drafting pencil. Then sawdust in the seams
of his clothes for weeks. In his knuckle-grooves,

she finds paint spatter. The smell of wood stain
where she kisses his neck. She is learning the cycles

of his season. On Monday, he tore down
two months' work. The smoking oven

that swallowed the witch, the Doric columns,
the house that spun to Oz—now scrap metal

and plaster and loose wood. Last show's lead
left town for the next circuit. Another pretty girl

will show up soon with an affinity for hot can lights
and the watchers beyond the proscenium arch.

Yes, this wife is learning her husband's work.
In his pockets, she finds hammered nails ripped out

by the same hand that drove them in. Already
he's sketching new uses for the lumber, pine undersides

still covered with the pencil markings of the last build.
A whole past he has taught himself to forget.

PULL

Home. Home past Ohio,
past the farmhouse
in which I infant-dreamed

and learned to crawl.
Past even the full sea
of my mother's belly. Back

to a few weathered mountains
rising along the north fork
of the Kentucky and a story

that's somewhere, happening
still—my mother
in the front bedroom

of her grandmother's house on a hill.
My mother just a bob-haired girl
and the pinpoint of me riding deep.

The next mountain burning
and the lace curtain snaking
in her smoke-churned dreams.

MY FATHER'S RIVER ROADS

We ride Route 52 home past RV camps
    called Poker Flat and Moon Hollow,

past towns like Felicity and Utopia, each
    with its church spire, its tavern, its IGA.
        Each with its Saturday-slow auto shop.

All the while, the Ohio shows ragged
    through the trees, cold and heron-grey.

The afternoon spent in cemeteries
    connecting family lines to a Revolutionary man
        named Valentine Peers, my father's father in his plot

nearly thirty years and my grandmother's name
    already etched onto the slab, my father drives

too fast. At the river bend, we pass a barge
    slugging upstream, and ahead, a ferry bears
        the lone car on its deck from one bank to the next.

GATHERING

listening to Andrei Ivanovich play Chopin's "Sonata No. 2 in B-Flat Minor"

Before the boy vanishes, before
he even slips his feet into the skates,

the crust of pond ice fissures.
A low sound, like the slow rip of denim.

Before thunder roils overhead, all
kettle crash and doom—the storm

already come, already half-gone—
a woman at a sink of soapy water

wipes her brow to a distant rumble.
Feel how the energy pulses, far-off,

gathering, how knots of crocuses hum
before their petals fan into January corollas.

How a mouse on its hind legs twitches
its nose at the oats laid out, its reflection

in the shine of the spring-loaded bar.
How in foreplay, before the foregone,

fingers climb the knobs of a naked spine,
and in the opening bars

of Chopin's *marche funèbre*, a foot presses
the *una corda* pedal, the piano's steel strings

tight-lipped and trembling—

YOU TELL ME OF THE WINTERS IN LARAMIE

And it's the lot out behind the funeral home
that catches me, those boyhood afternoons
you and your brother spent at the cusp
of a frozen wildflower field where piles
of plowed snow hulked. David with his pick
and you with your shovel hollowing caves

into the mounds. Breath whorled blue on the air
before vanishing, the snow packed tight
from mooncap knees. Your father at work
on a sermon for Zion Lutheran, your mother's
tumors still unformed, you worked wordlessly,

as you do now, each chamber just large enough
to crawl into. Snow groaned all around.
At dusk, the sky taut as a wound's dressing,
you and David slipped back across the street
to fill buckets at the kitchen sink. Your loads
splashed into that day's cave, you were ready

for sleep, knowing water's nature—how
it would freeze overnight and solidify the snow.
Boys build forts which they keep long after
their forts' demise. Yours, husband, a glinting
chamber that could hold your body till spring.

LAKE OUACHITA, LATE SUMMER

You swim to the next cove, the only act
of leaving you can take here in the water's
flow. Kicking away, you shred the lake
into heavy white spray. I clutch an orange raft,
poor swimmer, and float. I half know
to follow you after a fight, half know to let you

go. The rented pontoon, tied to a sapling,
grinds its metal base against the pebbled shore.
Islands litter the waterscape, hilltops before
they dammed the river. Never cut, the forest
is still rooted below. The guidebook says
striped bass, bream, and freshwater jellyfish slip

through the canopy. I'm good at thinking
of these other things—the drone of motorboats,
the whir and zip of brooch-sized dragonflies.
It's mating season for them. After that
comes death. We are weeks from our first anniversary,
weeks from moving into a house we'll hate,

weeks from all the other weeks we can't
anticipate. You return in the form of a head
bobbing up through the water's glare.
Near me again, you keep your jaw clenched,
and I take your hand, but not too quick.
In spite of myself, I want to kiss your shoulders,

already over-pink. Instead, I balance my foot
on the stub-end of a drowned tree that stretches
its blanched trunk who knows how far down,
and you take hold of my raft. We don't speak.
There's a metaphor here, perhaps, but we're still
too awestruck at what we've done to know.

"A HOUSE UPON THE HEIGHT—"

—Emily Dickinson

The fence that runs the road hems the house in,
thigh-high grass and clover tight, pushing back
through the wire slats. The farmer's wife
next door says teenagers used to trespass

and do who knows what they do. *Call next time,*
she warns, *so I know who you are.* Great-granddaughter
of a man who grew up here, I haven't needed a place
to press my lips to other desperate lips in years.

Years, it looks, since kids have bothered trying—
the floorboards rotted out, windowpanes gone,
the siding like a salt-eaten wreck. The whole house,
sunk in its center, tugged under, the porch's edges

curling in June. And still I want to trace my fingers
through the dust of these closed and failing rooms.

HOLDING

My grandmother hands me her mother's ration book,
still lined with stamps. She hands me Victory Mail,
her brothers' cursive spilling like water over rocks.
Envelopes, whose edges have been eaten
by silverfish, addressed only to *The Cornetts, Blackey, Kentucky.*
She hands me an infantryman's pocket Gospel of John
and the stone of a story in which she's stringing beans
when, through the trees, she and her mother see
the boy on his bicycle coming, the boy bearing
a telegram that will announce her brother's release
from the POW camp. She hands me the mountainside
on which she and her eleven siblings were raised.
Photographs of grey children squinting into white sun.
Words like *coal tipple, broomcorn, field cradle.* The porch swing
on which she rocked back toward the house her father built
and out, almost past the edge, toward the Indian Bottom
where the schoolhouse sat. She hands me the river's
murmurations and, across, Aunt Bertie's orchard
where she could pull an apple down and bite.
A spilled churn, sheets boiled in lye and dancing white
on the line. She hands me a spring, somewhere
on the way to town, where a neighbor left a ladle out
for passersby. She hands me the relief of a cool drink.
In front of us sits the gold leaf trunk she's had restored,
the one her mother brought with her when she married
a century ago. *When was it made?* I ask. *Who knows,*
she shrugs. My grandmother puts her papers away.
I'm left with stories that will pill and alter in my hands.
That empty trunk. A broken ladle that I raise.

WHISKEY HAIRCUT

Saturday night, my husband and his brother tip
the bottle of Bushmills into their mouths.
They set up shop under the porch bulb's spill—
kitchen chair, old towel, the electric razor's trill.

My husband straightens his brother's neck
and slides the sheathed teeth up the stretch
of his occipital bone. Blonde hairs feather out
around them in the heat. I watch my husband's hand.

Steadiness is something I still haven't learned.
I fear nicks, uneven tufts, taking off too much
at once. Two years ago, my father-in-law
shaved his wife's head. "Chemo prep,"

she wrote in an email I wish I'd saved. I never
saw her that way. In my memory, she's still bangs
and a champagne bob, ends curled under, neat.
"Shave closer," my brother-in-law instructs,

mimicking his mother's undressing. I've feared
that too. God knows what's taken doesn't always
grow back. Trust—to bow and bare your head,
to let love's shaking hand shave you down.

MATING RITUALS OF THE BIOLUMINESCENT

Near a Malay village, male fireflies coruscate in synchrony,
thousands of *kelip-kelip* clustered on each mangrove,
blinking three abdominal blinks per second

to summon a mate. They pulse in unison, constellating
the river as tourists in the twilight reach their fingers
from boat railings to catch the low green glow.

***

Two or three days after a full moon, female Bermuda
glow worms rise from the island's sandy bottoms
and gather in the shallows. At fifty-six minutes

past sunset, they swim circles, spitting out their eggs
in emerald clouds. The large-eyed males arrive,
flashing and flashing, ejecting their sperm into the sea.

***

Before we married, I drove to his apartment, the sky ready
to rip into storm, curled birch leaves eddying against my car.
He stood in his door, the frame of his narrow body

framed, the world gone dark, a strobe light beating white
behind him, and I swear he looked like lightning then,
his fevered flicker drawing me up, licking me in.

IT'S NOT THE BED THAT'S A BOAT

but our sleep. On a rumple
        of waves, two loosed canoes.

One night I'll find you
        in your wooden ribs.

I'll tie a rope. I'll climb on.

VANISHING POINT

After you leave for work, I pack boxes and teach myself
to name. Red-bellied woodpeckers wear checkerboard wings,

and tufted titmice sing "Peter" three times. Mourning doves
shoot from the fence, wings whistling, their low coos

from the pines, needles shuddering like chimes of light.
Dragonflies and red wasps loop through the air,

and every time I tack another signifier to its signified,
a spider sidles across the patio, faster than

centipede grass quivers, too fast to recognize. I think
that's why spiders frighten me. There's too much

to lose through the needle's eye, and I've only looked
when it's time to leave—hornet nests like mummified faces

hanging from the eaves, clover whispering up our calves,
weeds thick as saplings. Barn swallows that dip and flap,

dip and flap, between the high trees at dusk.
A porch ceiling's worth of crane flies. We are two breaths

among millions—and I am nearly breathless. Come evening,
I sit outside facing the dogwoods and honeysuckles

and all the plain, unfragrant trees I haven't learned to name
until night like a tide takes the cinquefoil's last flare.

THE DOORWAY EFFECT

*Investigating that phenomenon of short-term memory in which we suddenly forget
what we were about to do, University of Notre Dame researchers recently determined
that we are more likely to forget when we walk through a doorway than when we
stay within the space of one room. They are calling this the "doorway effect."*

Gates and jumped chain-link. A tree-branched
doorway into belilaced woods. Tudor arches, too.

Whooshing revolving doors and the doorway
my parents added between rooms. My bedroom window

slipped through. Covered bridges, steel truss.
Turnstiles and vestibules. Each stanza a room

with a doorway to enter and a doorway to leave.
County lines marked with green signs. The tunnel

of every long drive. All of these—to pass through.
Escape and banishment, too. It's forgetting

that stays the same. Crossing means potential
loss, means what's left can never be regained,

and though it's already too late, I want
to turn back through all the rooms, opening

every door—single-leaf, garden, screen, and French.
All to stop the doors ahead, the heavy doors.

The lids on the boxes that cannot be raised.

DRIVING THROUGH THE VALLEY OF
THE SHADOW OF LOCUST TREES

What trees are these? I ask my father, their clusters
of boisterous white blooms turning the highway
into a bridal aisle. The flowers seem
as new to me as if they'd never threaded
the hills, as if the trees hadn't been there
unfolding their spindles all along.
In a few hours, my grandfather will be buried
in Kentucky's kiln-red clay. Death is new, too,
though I know it like a barge on the water—

the ripples on their way. I've never stood next
to a body's last breath, though I am twenty-six
and ashamed. *Locust trees*, my father claims.
A *white trail leading us*, I think.
But we cross the Ohio, steely in the early light,
and the locusts disappear with the valley's rise.
The rest of the way is a lonely, more somber drive.

EXPOSURE TIME

Out through the maple and pin oak shade,
through those thousand shaking slivers of light,

my sister and I hauled folding chaise lounges
to the backyard's one brilliant column of sun.

Stripping off our shorts and tees, wrenching open
the chairs, we laid our bodies in the blaze.

The nylon strips our mother wove anew each June
held tight to their metal frames, suspending us.

Always in summer, somewhere in that neighborhood,
a mower growled, the air laced with cut grass

and gasoline, barbed with the saw-whine of sweat bees
whose metallic bodies zipped between our own—

breasts wrapped in the triangles of our bikini tops, beads
of sweat pooling on the upper lip, in the clavicle's ditch.

We said nothing, those bees like shared and pinging thoughts.
Grass whispered up the chair legs, clover to twist

between finger and thumb. Girlhood is half wait, half
collective dream. Every twenty minutes, we rolled

our bodies over, surrendering them side by side. *Ready us,*
we willed the Ohio sun. We didn't know for what.

INFINITY IN AN INCH

The old house is different in the pictures. Here,
　　my mother and father, young, in the farmhouse kitchen.
　　　　Dishes stacked on wooden shelves my father nailed

in place. An economy bottle of Dawn
　　on the counter with a baker's dozen other
　　　　common things—dishrag, dirty mug, rolling pin.

Only the laminate looks right, an intricate
　　and yellowed leitmotif of flower and vine locked
　　　　in the honeycomb of my mind from those early years

of trawling the pantry floor. My memories
　　are eyes trained too tight—a kerosene lamp lighting
　　　　its sphere of the hundred-years cellar, a small door

tucked behind the landing's bookcase.
　　A keyboard lid I lifted and the piano's mouth
　　　　of keys. Dollhouse rooms with spaces my fingers

couldn't reach. Millefleurs wallpaper curling
　　at its seams, stairs that fell with the pull of a string.
　　　　A gold plate of spare change and the bathtub's claw feet.

Even the pictures outside retell a past I thought I knew—
　　my siblings and I holding hands in front of scrawny pines,
　　　　the road to town just behind. The yard's plainer

than it seemed. I could swear a forest loomed
　　over the one acre my father mowed, paths
　　　　tumbling into a density of pin oak sheaves

and serrated vines where yellow ropes of snakes dangled
　　and a spring house lay buried deep. Infinity in an inch.
　　　　In the grass stalk's dewdrop eye, ten thousand leaves.

That house, to me, a twilit dwelling, windows bright
      and the edges dissolving. Add it to all the old stories
           I love and believed—archetypal, happening forever,

out of reach and practicality. Now my mother talks
      of bed skirts she feared might brush the radiators and ignite.
           Hunters who stumbled across our yard, crosshaired the
                dogs.

A rat in the cellar she called my father home from work
      to kill. In the pictures, there are cake-streaked birthday plates.
           There are curtains—white as reverie—she must have washed.

                                      —after Rilke

ODYSSEY

We begin *in medias res*, three bodies piled
in the hull and our mother dragging

another squeaking cart behind to load.
She navigated whole mountainsides

of broccoli and romaine, mist-draped capes.
Walls of corn spilled silk. Dams of clementine

and Granny Smith, scales dangling from chains.
Nets brimmed with their catch—dirt-flecked russets

and onions offering their skins. Further in,
we passed the murky tank in which lobsters

sank and only their whiskers waved. Strait
after strait and the scroll of a list. Oil of Olay,

canned fish. Arctic lands and pitchers of milk.
We sailed wide of the butchers' island,

forewarned by bloody smocks. Rudder
of our mother's hand. At the whirlpool,

we dropped coins, copper discs spiraling
into the donation bin. Bakers in paper hats

held out loaves hot with breath to lure us.
Last, when the conveyor belt tugged

toward the cashier, and the bagger loaded
stalks and cans as furiously as bailing water,

our mother signed the check, delivering
us all with the arrow of her pen.

HAIBUN FOR THE GRANTHAM
STATION PLATFORM

That summer, island-strange and out of sync, I mapped myself—
heather-heavy moorland to the north, the Fens just east. I sat
at the station on clouded afternoons, the metal bench cold
beneath the corrugated overhang. My fingers clenched their
cardboard coffee cup. The clock's numbers flipped their white
legs on their board, East Coast trains squealing in from King's
Cross. Nottingham lay down the latticework of track to the right,
Peterborough left, and every hour, another train ambled east on
the Poacher Line.

When the numbers ripened and the air grew unsteady, I stepped
out into a sky netted with cable, the world just lines curving out
of sight. The hum became a whir became a roar, and at the lip of
yellow paint, as near to the platform edge as I could stand, I let
that express train bullet by.

> *Its wind opened my throat,*
> *a ravishing, and day-old papers*
> *fluttered in its wake.*

AT SKEGNESS

Day-tripper, I followed the crowd down Lumley Road
    past fish-and-chip stalls and postcard stands.

Where the pavement slumped in sand, no horizon
    focused through the North Sea fog—only carnival songs

to scratch the brume. I trudged thirty opaque meters,
    then the ocean swirled like a ghost at my feet. Boreal spray

on my neck, my braid wet, the most northerly water
    I'd ever seen. No one followed me out. I stood

and breathed. What is it about the ocean—the waves' lap
    and retreat, their low moon-pulled hum? I'd always believed

we learn ourselves in what we see. And this—a largeness
    hidden from me. Back at the station, I waited coldly

for the Midlands train. My body swayed as if rocked by—no,
    there's the lie. My rocking body was not moved by, was nothing like,

the soft violence that churns the sea. Nothing called to me.

PLUCK

Michigan cranberries and half pecks
of yellow Krispies weighted the tables

in the storeroom barn. Cider spiced
my siblings' corn-husk hair. The woodstove

smoldered and spent its fuel, my fingers tracing
knotted gourds. I shook with the cold's

breath on the back of my neck, each day's
darkening. Outside, the orchard's hills

shuddered toward sleep. Root-choked caverns,
I imagined, that might open like a wound

and swallow. But above, apples spilled
from trees. Late crop, bountiful and heedless

to the surety of frost. *Be brave, be brave,*
they whispered, chill to the touch.

THE NEW POETRY INSTRUCTOR

Yesterday, she asked for a poem
about a first-time experience,
unaware so many'd pick the same.
Her blouse like plastic wrap
against her back, she backpedals now,

sirening the dangers of the sentimental
and cliché—but she's just more
June drone. The students will write
what they want, their cogs stuck
on keeping two wheels upright,

how it felt to raise the dirt
and part mosquitoes in their wake.
Each poem ends the same: the sudden
down-hard and the knee like a peeled grape.
And even as she speaks, the instructor

remembers—McCoy Park's
two diamonds, all umber dust
in summer. The ground root-choked
near second base, her father's hand
gripping the seat, her body bumping along

in the after-dinner heat. Then release,
velocity coating her cheeks. How after
she tumbled left, the pedal spiked her calf.
How she'd like it back—her father
already running, help just behind.

INSTRUCTIONS FOR RETURN

Follow the serpentine river roads
toward the Little Miami's lip. Pass
    through the sycamores, their molting
whitewashed limbs. These are curves
    I can still ride hard, roads
I can trace along a back's bare skin.
    Feel that wind, saturated, undercut
with vespertine chill. Let it frizz
    your hair. Turn up the Smashing
Pumpkins or the Cowboy Junkies.
    That's river musk on your teeth. See
how the lightning bugs burn their bulbs
    just ahead? In the rearview, bats unstitch
your wake. Now the humming bridge
    in your fingertips and thighs.
Remember that darkening vein underneath,
    how it pushes and pushes toward
main stem waters. The truss will bear
    your weight ten thousand times.

LAST DAYS

I wake to the curtain blowing out, watery light
thrown across our limbs, the wind sucking the curtain
back in. Wordless minutes, I watch that jellyfish,
its slow propulsion.

Where will you take us?

Other days—

Let us be still.

TUESDAY EVENING

Another chartered jet from the airport
    next door shadows the driveway,

        the sky near the horizon cherry-red,
           over-kissed. Today, dozens

of crows squawked from tree to tree.
    In a poem I read, the birds were leaves

        returning to the trees. But today,
           the birds kept blowing away.

We are leaving this town soon.
    You are at the University, lighting

        another pageant for the undergrad girls
           who wear gowns that cost more

than my chain-store wedding dress,
    who smile into satin spotlights.

        Earlier, you sat on the bathtub's ledge
           as I cupped your ear and snipped the hairs

around it. You were half-turned, one arm
    circling my thigh. I pinched the cut hairs

        and blew them into the tub
           where hundreds more were spread.

You looked up at me with a look that meant
    I could take you then. I wish I had.

        Tomorrow is a road we'll ride, and each
           fanned hair's a wish. I wish us well.

NOTES

"A House upon the Height—": The title is taken from Emily Dickinson's poem #399.

"Whiskey Haircut" is written in memory of my mother-in-law, Barbara Schroeder.

"Driving Through the Valley of the Shadow of Locust Trees" is written in memory of my grandfather Walter Strunk.

"Infinity in an Inch": The phrase "twilit dwelling" is taken from Rainer Maria Rilke's letter to a young poet dated February 17, 1903: "And even if you were in a prison whose walls allowed none of the sounds of the world to reach your senses—would you not still have always your childhood, that precious, royal richness, that treasure house of memories? Turn your attention there. Try to raise the submerged sensations of that distant past; your personality will grow stronger, your solitude will extend itself and will become a twilit dwelling which the noise of others passes by in the distance." From *Letters to a Young Poet*, translated by Reginald Snell (Mineola, NY: Dover, 2002), p. 12-13.

ABOUT THE AUTHOR

Corinna McClanahan Schroeder received her MFA from the University of Mississippi and is currently a PhD candidate at the University of Southern California, where she holds a Wallis Annenberg Endowed Fellowship. She is the recipient of an AWP Intro Journals Award in poetry, and her poems have been published in numerous journals, including *The Gettysburg Review*, *Shenandoah*, *Tampa Review*, *Poet Lore*, and *Blackbird*. Originally from Cincinnati, Ohio, she lives with her husband, Matthew, in Los Angeles, California.